MARIAN ANDERSON

AMAZING OPERA SINGER

Famous African Americans

Patricia and
Fredrick McKissack

Enslow Elementary
an imprint of

Enslow Publishers, Inc.
40 Industrial Road
Box 398
Berkeley Heights, NJ 07922
USA

http://www.enslow.com

For Mrs. Evelyn Glore-Ashford

Enslow Elementary, an imprint of Enslow Publishers, Inc.

Enslow Elementary® is a registered trademark of Enslow Publishers, Inc.

Original edition published as *Marian Anderson: A Great Singer* in 1991.

Library of Congress Cataloging-in-Publication Data

McKissack, Pat, 1944-
  Marian Anderson : amazing opera singer / Patricia and Fredrick McKissack.
    p. cm. — (Famous African Americans)
  Includes index.
  Summary: "A simple biography for early readers about Marian Anderson's life"—Provided by publisher.
  ISBN 978-0-7660-4101-1
  1. Anderson, Marian, 1897-1993—Juvenile literature. 2. Contraltos—United States—Biography—Juvenile literature. 3. African American singers—Biography—Juvenile literature. I. McKissack, Fredrick. II. Title.
  ML3930.A5M42 2012
  782.1'092—dc23
  [B]

2012007618

Future editions
Paperback ISBN 978-1-4644-0202-9
ePUB ISBN 978-1-4645-1115-8
PDF ISBN 978-1-4646-1115-5

Printed in the United States of America

10 9 8 7 6 5 4 3 2 1

082012 Lake Book Manufacturing, Inc., Melrose Park, IL

To Our Readers: We have done our best to make sure all Internet Addresses in this book were active and appropriate when we went to press. However, the author and the publisher have no control over and assume no liability for the material available on those Internet sites or on other Web sites they may link to. Any comments or suggestions can be sent by e-mail to comments@enslow.com or to the address on the back cover.

♻ Enslow Publishers, Inc., is committed to printing our books on recycled paper. The paper in every book contains 10% to 30% post-consumer waste (PCW). The cover board on the outside of each book contains 100% PCW. Our goal is to do our part to help young people and the environment too!

Photo Credits: Courtesy Everett Collection, pp. 16, 20; Library of Congress, pp. 1, 3, 4; Schomburg Center for Research in Black Culture/The New York Public Library/Astor, Lenox and Tilden Foundations, p. 13.

Illustration Credits: Ned O., pp. 7, 8, 10, 14, 18.

Cover Photo: Library of Congress

Words in bold type are are explained in Words to Know on page 22.

Series Consultant:
Russell Adams, PhD
Emeritus Professor
Afro-American Studies
Howard University

CONTENTS

Marian Anderson's love of music began at an early age. She grew up to become a world-famous singer.

CHAPTER 1
SING, MARIAN, SING

Marian Anderson was born in Philadelphia, Pennsylvania, on February 27, 1897. Her father sold coal in the winter and ice in the summer. Her mother cleaned houses. The Andersons went to church every Sunday.

Mr. Robinson was in charge of the children's **choir** at Union Baptist Church. He invited Marian to join the choir. She was just six years old. And so began her love of music.

Marian grew up singing in church. She learned the old slave songs called **spirituals**. She sang alone and with others. Music filled her with happiness. Singing was almost as wonderful as going to the circus . . . almost.

One day, Marian heard music coming from a window. She peeked inside. A dark-skinned woman was playing a piano in her living room. Marian was excited. She felt proud to see a woman who had dark skin like hers playing so beautifully. Marian knew then that if she wanted to, she could learn to play the piano, too.

Marian's family was poor. When her father died, they became even poorer. But Marian didn't mind working. She scrubbed her neighbor's front steps for a penny or two. She sang all the time. Her neighbors loved to hear her sing as she worked.

Marian's family did not have a lot of money. They all had to work hard. Marian liked to sing as she worked.

A mean woman once told Marian she could not take singing lessons because she was black. Marian did not let this stop her.

CHAPTER 2

MI-MI-MI-MI-MI-MI-MI

Marian and her sisters, Alyce and Ethel, played together and went to school together. When they were in high school, they began wondering what they would do when they were grown up. Would they be doctors? Lawyers? Teachers, as their mother once had been?

More than anything else, Marian wanted to sing. But could a poor, black girl from Philadelphia sing well enough to make a living? Yes, she decided, it was possible.

Marian went to a nearby music school. She could hear singing.

Mi-Mi-Mi-Mi-Mi-Mi-Mi

"What do you want? We don't teach colored people," a woman told Marian. "Go away!"

Giuseppe Boghetti heard something special in Marian's voice. He agreed to teach her.

The words were unkind and mean. Marian felt bad—
not for herself, but for the woman. How could a person
love music and be so filled with hate? she thought.

At last, Marian found someone who was willing to teach
her—Mary Saunders Patterson, her first voice teacher.
Marian worked hard at her lessons. Soon she was singing
her **scales**.

One day, Marian had a chance to sing for Giuseppe
Boghetti, who was a very well-known music teacher.
He was too busy to take a new **student**. "But I will listen to
her sing," he said. Marian sang "Deep River" for him.

Then, after hearing Marian sing, Boghetti smiled.
He said she had a lot of talent. Boghetti said he would take
one more student: Marian Anderson.

CHAPTER 3
HIGH AND LOW TIMES

Marian had happy times as well as sad times in her life. One bad time came in 1924, when she was twenty-seven years old.

Marian studied very hard with Giuseppe Boghetti. She had sung at churches in Philadelphia. Her voice was strong. She was good—very good. Everybody said so. Why not sing in New York?

Boghetti said she would need to work even harder to be ready for such a **concert**.

Marian liked the idea of singing in a big music hall— like Town Hall in New York City. So that is where Marian had her first New York concert.

Even though she had a good voice, Marian's first New York concert was not a big success.

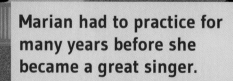

Marian had to practice for many years before she became a great singer.

It was a terrible flop! Very few people came. The newspapers said, "Marian Anderson has a good voice. . . but she needs more **practice**."

Marian knew they were right. And Boghetti made her practice. She sang high **notes**, low notes, and all the notes in between. Learning how to sing well was hard work.

Her practice soon paid off. In 1925, Marian won a prize for singing. She won a chance to sing a solo with the New York **Philharmonic** Orchestra in August.

She was good—very good. It felt great! She sang the high notes, the low notes, and all the notes in between. She had never sung them better.

Even though she was a star, Marian never forgot to thank the people who had helped her.

CHAPTER 4
Brava! Brava!

· ·

Marian went to Europe at the end of 1927. Her first major European concert was in Germany in early 1930. People cheered for her. Brava! Brava! The crowds cheered.

Next Marian sang in Denmark, Sweden, Norway, and Russia. Her voice was better than ever. She was very well known. But not many people in the United States had heard her sing. It was time to come home.

A concert was set for December 30, 1935, at Town Hall in New York City. On the boat trip home, Marian broke her leg. The show must go on, she told her family and friends.

Only a few people knew her leg was broken. This time Town Hall was full. Marian stood behind the piano. She wore a long, blue dress.

Marian sang in cities all over the world.

It was very quiet. The music began. Her leg hurt, but Marian sang and sang! When she was done, everyone burst into cheers.

Marian sang all over the United States. She sang in the South, where laws ruled that black people and white people had to live separately. They could not go to school together, work or play together. They could not sit together on buses or in music halls.

Whenever Marian sang before a crowd in the South, she bowed to the black people first. That was her way of showing she cared. It also showed that she was proud of her race. Brava! Brava! They cheered for her.

CHAPTER 5
OH, WHAT A MORNING!

. . . .

Marian sang at the White House for **President** Franklin D. Roosevelt and First Lady Eleanor Roosevelt. Mrs. Roosevelt also invited Marian's mother to the White House.

Howard University invited Miss Anderson to sing in Washington, D.C., in 1939 at Constitution Hall. But a group called the Daughters of the American Revolution (DAR), who owned the hall, said no black person could sing there.

Marian was sad—not for herself, but for the Daughters of the American Revolution.

Other people were very angry about the way a great American was being treated. One was Mrs. Roosevelt. She quit the DAR to let the world know she didn't like the way Miss Anderson was treated.

Singing at the Lincoln Memorial was very special to Marian. It was one of many honors that she received throughout her life.

Then, on Easter Sunday morning in 1939, Marian Anderson sang in Washington, D.C. Oh, what a morning!

She stood on the steps of the Lincoln Memorial and sang the **National Anthem** before 75,000 people of all races. As always, a Marian Anderson concert ended with the spirituals she learned as a child. She sang "My Soul Is Anchored in the Lord." It was very beautiful. Some people cried.

In her long career, Marian won many honors and made many records. She sang for crowds all over the world. In 1955, she became the first African American to sing a leading part at the well-known Metropolitan Opera in New York City. She also sang at the March on Washington in 1963, where Dr. Martin Luther King, Jr., gave his "I Have a Dream" speech. Oh, what a morning! She even got to sing at Constitution Hall.

Marian Anderson **retired** on April 19, 1965, after a concert at New York's Carnegie Hall. In February 1993, Marian celebrated her ninety-sixth birthday. In April, she died.

She will be remembered as a person who brought people together through music.

Words to Know

choir—A musical group; a group of singers, sometimes in a church.

concert—A musical show.

national anthem—The song of a country. The national anthem of the United States is "The Star-Spangled Banner."

note—A musical sound; a music symbol that shows the musician what sound to make. When put together, notes make music.

philharmonic orchestra—A large group of musicians who play concerts for audiences.

practice—To go over and over something until it is learned well.

president—The leader of a country or group.

retired—No longer working.

scales—Musical sounds that move higher or lower note by note. Singers practice scales before singing.

spirituals—Religious songs that were first sung by African-American slaves.

student—A person who is interested in learning.

22

LEARN MORE

BOOKS

Braun, Eric. *Marian Anderson*. Mankato, Minn.: Capstone Press, 2005.

Ryan, Pam Munoz. *When Marian Sang: The True Recital of Marian Anderson*. New York: Scholastic, 2002.

Sutcliffe, Jane. *Marian Anderson*. Minneapolis: Lerner Publishing, 2007.

WEB SITES

Marian Anderson: A Life in Song
<http://www.library.upenn.edu/special/gallery/anderson/index.html>

Marian Anderson Biography
<http://www.afrovoices.com/anderson.html>

INDEX

J
B
M

Anderson

McKissack, Pat.

Marian Anderson.

DATE			

FEB   2013   BAKER & TAYLOR